good deed rain

and Light

Paul S. Piper

and Light ©2016 Paul S Piper & Good Deed Rain
Bellingham, Washington
ISBN 978-1-68419-381-3
Writing: Paul Piper
Cover: Penny Piper
Watercolors: Penny Piper
Author photo: Clarissa Mansfield
Production Assistance: Fred Sodt

Prelude

I have never done this before, but a word about these poems might be welcomed by the reader. They are collected from the past four years, and represent a number of styles I was working in, and continue to work in: lyric, impressionistic, objectivist, nature and spiritual (many of these influenced by Chinese and Japanese nature and spiritual poetry), a few of social protest, and some that went bump in the night and landed on the page.

I am responsible for them all, and at better times could probably be held for treason or aesthetic idiocy by the poetry police. Do not doubt they exist.

The poems strive to be honest and a record or journal of my life, soul and mind. Any failings are entirely my own.

I thank Allen Frost for pretty much everything about this book, and may his selfless spirit live on forever. I thank my very talented sister for her watercolors which grace these pages. I thank my very great friends for being part of the milieu, my wife Joan for her love, my poetry group, Chuck Luckmann and Tim Pilgrim, for their insight and rigor. And I thank my muse who is out there somewhere smiling sublimely.

I

Poem for David Taylor

The moon is an opalescent shell
a child picks up and puts

to her ear, and hears
the end and beginning

of time roaring
through her mind

The Cat

The wind at dusk
is kicking up, and the cat

gazes from the porch
and sees what we cannot

and purrs her soft words
that are not words

Poem for Allen

Drops of rain, teardrops,
cottonwood leaf, big

yellow heart. I stick
my hand into its pocket

and pull out a new day
along with some lint

which I stuff in my pillow
where the new night sleeps

Sunlight

Sunlight ignites tears
of rain on the rusty fence
then cloud shadow
and fat drops of rain
and the rest of my life

And Light

And light comes to this land
yet again, yet again

we have enough to go on, light
coming its great distance

to this land, and that
is all we truly know

that it comes bursting
or dragging days and that

is all we truly know and
it is enough

Moths

Evening moves hard to dark
and air fills with tiny white moths.

Our eyes candle them
but like they to fire, we

dare not range too close.
Weightless on furred gossamer

wings they make love in air,
chaotic and dizzy they dance

flitter, leap and swoop
silently in this night until

the wind erupts and they are gone,
leaving us alone with our visions,

our human weight.

What I Fear

What I fear is hidden
by the dark but what i
fear most is hidden by
the light

Hunger

There is deep stillness
in the sadness that is
this dark pond as evening
falls and the swallows cut
sky and crimson clouds
fade. Then I walk back
out of stillness
into what is equally infinite
within us all, that
unassailable hunger.

The Cold

Yesterday thousands of snow geese
in the Skagit fields, this morning

small flocks passing south
out of British Columbia, braying

in the cold Frasier air.
My breath huffing white clouds

that stun in morning light, then
vanish. A single deer hoof print

frozen in clay, clear as any word,
clearer. All words can do is point

at things we'll never truly know,
leave us on the ground, looking up.

Rhododendrons

Soft rain, dawn gray
cleansed. Walking quiet,

muted
the way a trumpet player

mutes,
then breaks loose with joy –

the red rhododendrons.

The Blue Hour

Outside the blue hour
has arrived

and the wayward birds straighten
their path home

Olsen Creek
for Jack Duffy

Icicle teeth on logs crossing Olsen Creek,
dog wild with cold, chasing sticks
into the water, splashing
furiously, shaking his head. Crows
cawing, flapping across cobalt sky.
Alder barren of leaves in morning sun.
The sound of a chainsaw starting in
far away. Everything far away, so
close.

At My Cabin up the Swan

Finally the chores are done,
soft breeze, evening sun. Water

hauled, dinner prepped and
cooked. These three trout I've caught

a blessing. It is their suffering, their
death I eat, now they swim in my

body. As someday I will feed others
my suffering and body. But for now

let chilled wine be poured. I toast
the patient earth who waits

and cares little of time.

Day after George's Death

Storms sweep from the coast
voices on the phone

ghosts luminous in the air
around us, all those

lost. Birds carve us.
Our breath is given, taken

away. We are finally
breathless.

A New Land

after hours of heavy rain
the sun breaks miraculous, scouring
us with its brilliance, leaving us
as tendrils, dripping and naked
in a new land

Right Currency

Wind blows cottonwood leaves to silver
but when we try to spend them
they twist and turn to green hearts

Storm

Thunder closer, a single bird
calls
into quickening wind

Untitled

This infinite departure –
rain dripping in the dark
from the plum tree

Conversing with Chickadees

The winds pick up
as I sit conversing

with Chickadees
busy with gossip

in the plum tree
the sweet peas dried out

yet several flare white
against the old cedar fence.

The Moon

the moon, the
moon, how many

times can you say
it in a row without

asking how many
reasons to live? the

moon, the
moon, how many

are there? the
beautiful horror

that is
the moon?

Red Tulips

Along the deserted road
red tulips startle the rain

Across the world horses
break into a river

sending a spray of water
into the sun

Postcard of Light

lichen and aged cedar leaves burn
in slat of sun through trees

postcard of morning sent
light years ago, arriving now saying

wake up
sleepy head

Stopping on the Corner

My dog Django stops
every walk to eat straw grass
at the corner and every walk
I pull him away and up
the hill. It is my lie
that I have something better
to do, that I need to hurry, that
I should not stay on that corner
watching him eat grass
in the patient sunlight,
forever.

Fish

I ask the old man
where the fish are.
"Right here" he says
pointing at the hard, dusty
ground. "You have to dig
down far, far, to the pure
cold water."

Prayer

Crow's wings catch sun
flash black to gold as
it lands on top a pole
and folds them to its body
in silent prayer

Socks

An old pair of white socks, limp
on the clothes line between two
fir, glowing in the early sun

Autumn

White mushrooms break
the veil of grass their
spores in the wind
the earth quivers
with the quiet fury
of Autumn

Mist

The fir disappear in mist
and thus are kissed are almost
gone but for the black echo
of the crow gliding out

Haiku Variants

Cottonwood leaf
golden heart abandoned
on black asphalt street

More, many yellow hearts
floating in the pond
love lost in water

Dark night, black room
tiny glint of light
moon reflecting off metal cup

Granite peaks blurred
by smoke. Fire eats
forests miles away.

Words so inept at times
tiny creatures flailing in space
legs, wings barely touching anything

Blackberry tart bursts open --
Glottal food

the sound of water
striking water –
one sound or two?

A Chathamesque evening
a manslaughter of crows
chase the day west

To Turn Me Over

I was on edge as any war
but the lake refused to end and
with its reflection turning
sent me over

Neil's Grave, Pony Creek, Montana

Limpid pools hidden
by dense brush

Last night coyotes
howling, cold skin

and stars brutal
and brilliant

fire in its circle
a warm orange heart

and upstream my brother-in-law
Neil buried in the hillside

near the barbed wire fence
and the curious, smiling cows

Eating Bone

Eating bone
with an ash fork

plate of
turquoise sky

red sand and sand
and weathered rock

sun the solo eye
of day, moon

night's winking
eye

coyotes
just

doing it
everywhere

wild

Two Eagles
for Robert Sund

two eagles circling
above Haggen's parking lot
looking for really tiny cars

II

The Other Side of Time

The Indian Plum are blooming
at Whatcom Falls, and snow flakes
larger than a baby's hand drift
from invisible sky. I imagine
I am moving backwards
through the forest at night
and the soft call of a thrush
touches me but I know it is you,
my star over me.

Untitled

I'm looking for something that isn't here, in
this line or the next, rather it's ahead looking
back, or lived before this investigation began.
For the sake of discussion let's call it cyclamen.
Let's imagine it lives in a pot, with a distracting
dress of foil, and a large card leashed to its leaves.
"Call me beautiful" it blushes, pretending to faint.

Building

I am building a doorway to light
blasting stars in black schist

I am building a doorway into light of apostrophes,
asterisks, exclamation points, innuendo

I am building a doorway to light
rectilinear, sharp yet fluid as God

Paradox we are all
hammer, nail, axe and saw

I am building a doorway into light
a litany of a woman's perilous voice

etc.
All history unfolds before you

I am building….
but the window is stained, stuck, staring

straight at me, black eye of Cyclops
I am opening into light by walking

through a doorway I blasted into
your smile, your lovely smile

Hey You

I liked you better as a country lyric
than a toad frozen to a rock calling yourself art

touché though. I never asked what *you*
wanted.

Blue Commas
for Robert Creeley

Blue commas, red-
hot words, black

fluted mouth,
trumpet fire

not all yet not all
of it, something

more, something
else

Untitled

What do I know about you?
What do you know about me?

even OK the end
but

maybe there is another way, a left
turn illegal but necessary

to bring this ship
around and over

the horizon

My Baby, Still

The wind in the cottonwood leaves
over the laughing water

silver hearts a flappin crazy
in love, this way and that

it goes over the years, sometimes
standing still, sideways, backwards

even but mostly dancing
with my baby, still.

III

Letter from Montreal

Guys –

The group of students in Parc Mont-Royal
laugh, sing, shriek just above where I lie

on the grassy expanse. They are delirious,
delicious in their wild joy. Is it they don't know

the light will go out, or is the switch too close?
One woman, missing a tossed ball, groans

so close to sexual that I can hear her release,
how it will sound in that empty room. My

release no longer falls far. My cage has tightened.
Even the sky above me is made of words –

blue, white, grey, sun. So human
it is lost to me.

Poem for Jim Harrison

If deer peopled the streets
ears jammed with earbuds,

faces planted in phones, fingers
and thumbs stroking friends, texting

other lovers, bumping into posts, tripping
over curbs, wolves would be fat,

happy, not at all endangered.

Poem for Robert Creeley

For Love and what
else? It's that intricate terrain

mapped, and in the room
pregnant sounds of night,

breathing, rustlings,
and the outside

furious hymns of crickets;
moon in its crescent sleigh rides

behind the alpine fir.

My Office

The morning's sleet erupting from black sky
was a sign we have no control, and now

in the warmth of afternoon sun there
is not the expected joy, rather the hard curves

of an oak chair yielding to nothing except saw
and axe. We are surrounded

by mountains and sky and that is
the miniscule world. Beyond

is a cave that purges itself of finity,
where the light is held so tightly

in the fist of chaos it is crushed out.
Our concept of distance, even metaphor, is futile.

We are feeble creatures and yet
our hearts beat out against it, our

desire a desperate wish.

Two Micro Partitas for Allen

1

Three Buddhists from the conference
walking in front of me eating
ice cream cones, talking about how
consciousness is reborn

2

Two first grade boys sitting at a picnic
table at Boulevard Park discussing
what dog is used for hot
dogs, deciding finally on
collies

Futile Buddha #3

After the last storm passed leaving glazed
and broken fir, I notice the stone Buddha

head toppled, its face staring deeply
into the earth.

In looking more closely however, sensing
movement, I saw the head slowly banging

itself against the dirt in despair. Simply
too much human agony, suffering and deceit

to cope with.

Futile Buddha #4

Buddha douses himself with gas,
lights a match. Sitting upright
in perfect form, all desire, all
anger and sorrow burns away
leaving only light, then only
ash.

Early Morning

Early morning, stopping while the dog sniffs
I hear the trickling of water underground

deep where sorrow yawns; walking back into the call
of a barred owl, a moan, a black cat

bone; windows, yellow with light in the dark
hiding stories; maple leaf uncurled

as if a hand letting go; a soft eruption

I Am Ignorant More than Death

Heat stupefies. My skin burns, eyes
blur. The heat on water on watercolor.

It washes the world away.
Like a stone in a field

I lay dormant until released
in flight by the child I was

walking home from school. A
stone in flight. Death is more innocent

than I. Time will not remember
me yet I remember time.

Untitled

Three shirtless men are building a house
none will be able to afford.

One sights his hammer
along the edge of a turret, precisely

as sun ricochets off a tear in the flashing.
Beyond, a buzzard circles lazily.

The man feels its pull, the thick substance
of his life stirred

and the hammer falls to hang lightly
from his hand, and he laughs, and laughs

and laughs.

The Songs of Birds

The songs of birds are swimming
in a cobalt bowl. There is finality

to it, and also to the oak table
on which the bowl rests, as if

this had already occurred
in a life already lived.

The room has always been empty
but the windows open onto fields

rich with loam, virile weather
and bowed alfalfa. Bovine footprints

lead many ways, cluster around muddy
puddles, and the wind gusts, and gusts

again, and the liquid in the blue bowl
ripples. The light it catches flickers

on the white wall. And the songs
of birds swim on, undisturbed.

True Existence
> *True existence is only that which does not exist* Ge Fei

We hang
    among the cheap margarine-colored forsythia
        the Victoria Secret pink camellias

texting, sipping Bellinis. Provence
    is close in mind, those tourists
        crab-stepping up steep sharp

rocks chased by ocean. Beauty is a
    powder, a wink, a curve, a beat
        and sun beats

down. We are allowed our sins for we
    are young and own the world. We
        arc across the sky

ending at dawn. But when we are alone
    there is nowhere we can go to
        lose ourselves, even in this

circular garden, with strutting pigeons
    and crowds pushing, and a scrap
        of paper hanging precariously

over the fountain's edge, arms thrown wide. Then
    suddenly we are tired of the drama,
        and the fountains spouting off

and although the river only flows one way, we
    let ourselves go, and hope for the fury
        of waterfall to bury us beautiful.

The Stain

semen on my underwear, red
wine on the carpet, congealed grease
on the kitchen counter, the sun's afterimage
on the retina, black spot on
right lung, word on blank page
single cloud in a perfect sky
what I said when the time came
to say it

The Zen Chess Master

Like the zen chess master
he stood with his head off

years and miles away some-
thing happened God maybe

and there were cliffs of course
nine of them with names with lots

of consonants and lust but every-
body was cool when they threw them

off. Karma they called it but its more like
Fata Morgana getting her way.

Commentary on Khoa Hu

I am already dead
never reborn
although there is talk

but talk is cheap
as the booze served here

nothing but secrets
reborn as bats
who are they
anyway?

this way I have traveled
to absolute beauty
but it fractured
into infinite pieces

the land here is astral
yet penstemon and
valerian survive
and with them the hermeneutics
of silver-barked fir

so much for stopping
the wind
I am already dead
as I said

the birds
heard
are never seen

the sun also rises
when it wants to

We Are the World

The lovely young woman stalled
at the bus stop wears tanned Argentine cowhide
wrapped snugly around her feet
and sexy ankles; her necklace,
pearls torn from oysters in Java, hangs
loosely across the top of her breasts. Copper
bracelets mined on the backs of Peruvian miners
adorn her fashionably thin wrists. Egyptian
cotton sewn by a ten year old girl in Sri Lanka
falls just below her knees. Yak wool socks
knitted by Uyghurs hide under her boots. A white
silk scarf from Punjab, India, whose creator died
in a sweatshop fire, half-moons across her chestnut
hair. Her comb clip, amber from Tunesia,
an heirloom given by her mother when she left
for college, catches the sun and burns. Without
thinking of her mother, the girl impatiently stabs
at an IPhone manufactured in a Chegdu factory
warren; stabs and stabs the little letters, reaching out
to her newly silent boyfriend traveling in Tuscany.
And with no bus in sight she is suddenly lost
in the distance of the day.

IV

Father

Moments on fire
the pond edges

sedge-rimmed. Dog
relaxes, tosses his head,

eats grass. Evening
light uncanny, tricks

of shadow and loss.
Tomorrow

I pick up my father
at the airport, see

what the years have done
to he I so love.

Picking at the sores on his face
he has fierce eyes.

He wanted the years of his life
to end and when he didn't get that

he said fuck it, I might as well do
what I want, what the body is able.

But Able died under the jaw
of an ox and music no longer

comes in pieces that fit together.

I

My father has lost
his voice, his

language. Sentences
broken to words, words

into staggered sounds,
a rasp in the throat, tickle

of tongue, warm breath
on my ear as I bend in

to catch last meaning.
What message

this passage of air? What
passed between us? Heart

still beats, breath still pushes his chest
up and down, eyes glaucomic,

and rain everywhere cold
tears in the trees.

II

Today I fed my father applesauce
I would touch the spoon, a small

smooth spoon, to his lips
and if I was lucky he'd open

his mouth. Most of his lower teeth
missing, flecks of white spittle

like snow on a dark night path.
I'd place the spoon gently in his mouth

and he'd close down greedily, and
he wouldn't let go. Across the fields

there were three rifle shots in quick
succession. This was three days

before he left us.

III

Outside the windows, where he stares
From his hospice bed, are fields

of grass that he has, for the past year
mistaken for lakes. He talked about them

when we spoke on the phone. How

rough they were, how many people
were out fishing, how they were doing, what

the fish were biting on. It filled most of our
conversations. Shunning motors he preferred rowing,

taught me at a young age how to row and
steer large wooden and aluminum boats.

Sighting on a cabin or dock or lone
tree and keeping it center, knowing

what center was. The point wasn't getting
there fast, that would happen eventually,

but the rhythmic pull, the focused balance,
the strain of muscles in the back, shoulders,

arms, the burn of the sun, and the water
always the water, underneath.

IV

The white wings through the leaves
and the bell of a small train clanging

and how wind flattens the grass
all of it empty, a flat picture

I want to forget. All day the wind
off the ocean like a voice that says

nothing, roars nothing, over and
over again, saying nothing

can be said.

Untitled

The half-moon in the high corner
of the window passes through

as a white bird and sits with me
watching my father sleep

V

Oh and then came morning
as if always it would come, windows

open and curtains breathing as if
where we lived within what we called

house or home was in reality
a body of dust blown to the sun

VI

Spars of brilliant foxglove
and green, and the road curves

endlessly down. I stop where you
would have, along a river, by a large

eddy. Foam laces the seam. Copper
grass seed heads, yarrow, blackberry

flowers. The sound of the water
in the sky. I think I'm taking you

home but you're already here, waiting.

VII

The sun bright silver
on the water, and my father

is still dead. The branches of the pines
like so many greedy hands, grasping air,

letting nothing go, and the relentless waves
strike shore then feather

back. His hands are still
deep within me. Memory

is a crevice, the sea moving through
like wind through my hair, no end to it.

VIII

I have done that. I have cast
into the surf as the man below
the cliffs is doing, casting into froth
and reeling and repeating
and the waves gather
around him and the dark comes
in quick as the strike of a fish
feeding on the silver minnows
that were his eyes.

IX

There is an emptiness that wasn't there
before as if the air is thinner and there is
less of it

High up in the sky birds wheel
and curl and there is only silence
then that too is peeled away

X

I heard death knocking on my father's
door barging in picking up his frail chest

and smashing it to the hospice bed and he'd
gasp and gasp for a thread of air and death

would smash him again and this went on
four hours or more it was hard to get outside

time until finally death smiled and my father
lay calm

XI

My father never hiked Skyline Divide,
never sat in fields of lupine, buttercup,

and false hellebore; never saw the swarms
of tiny midges rising like early mist, felt

the overpowering pressure of sky
and mountains cragged and shouldered

and stuttered with snow, flat clouds
scudding north over British Columbia.

But I bring him with me today
where dark spars of fir pierce sky

and green is so poignant it stings and space
so vast my tears will never fill it.

XII

Birdsong, the front porch,
evening, dog asleep. Hard

to imagine it's been two weeks
since dad died. Time such a

distortion, immediate and gone,
the notes of a song I only now

notice has ceased.

Paul S. Piper was born and raised in Chicago, and lived for extensive periods in Montana and Hawaii. He received an MFA in Creative Writing from the University of Montana, Missoula, where he studied with Richard Hugo, William Kittredge, Richard Ford, and James Crumley among others. He is currently Special Collections Librarian at Western Washington University in Bellingham, Washington. He has several books of poetry – *White, Movement Apparent Song, Now and Then, Winter Apples*, and *Dogs and Other Poems*. He has one book of fiction, *South Fork and Other Stories*. He has also had the privilege of being included in the anthologies The *New Montana Story, America Zen* and *Tribute to Orpheus*. In addition he co-edited the book *Father Nature, X-Stories: The Personal Side of Fragile X Syndrome* and *A Flutter of Birds Passing Through Heaven: a Tribute to Robert Sund*.

Penny Piper was born in Chicago and has lived in Oregon for the past 35 years. She has painted, using watercolors, for the past 8 years. Although self-taught, she has the gift of painting both light and life. She is a wonderful caregiver, a passionate nature lover, and the mother of three fantastic children.

GOOD DEED RAIN

Saint Lemonade (Allen Frost, 2014)

Playground (Allen Frost, 2014)

Roosevelt (Allen Frost, 2015)

5 Novels (Allen Frost, 2015)

The Sylvan Moore Show (Allen Frost, 2015)

Town in a Cloud (Allen Frost, 2015)

A Flutter of Birds Passing Through Heaven: A Tribute To Robert Sund (edited by Allen Frost and Paul Piper, 2016)

At the Edge of America (Allen Frost, 2016)

Lake Erie Submarine (Allen Frost, 2016)

and Light (Paul S Piper, 2016)

Coming Soon:
A tribute to Clyde Sanborn